Be-going family Therapy

Be~good~to~your~family Therapy

written by
Kass Dotterweich

illustrated by
R.W. Alley

Abbey Press

Text © 1997 by Kass Dotterweich
Illustrations © 1997 by St. Meinrad Archabbey
Published by One Caring Place
Abbey Press
St. Meinrad, Indiana 47577

All rights reserved.
No part of this book may be used or reproduced in any manner without written permission of the publisher, except in the case of brief quotations embodied in critical articles and reviews.

Library of Congress Catalog Number
96-79960

ISBN 0-87029-300-1

Printed in the United States of America

Foreword

Family life is challenging. Changing values, overcrowded schedules, information overload, cultural and economic pressures all make it hard to be a family today.

Yet no single unit of society is as important as the family. For it's within the family that we are all fashioned into the persons we are. Our individual traits, our unique talents, our strengths can be enhanced in countless ways—or can be restricted, ignored, or repressed—within the family structure. And it's within the family that we learn to love ourselves, other people, and God.

Be-good-to-your-family Therapy provides simple but substantial direction for making your family life all it can be. And while pointing out the responsibilities each member has within the family, it will remind you of the wonders, the joys, the blessings, the privilege of being a family.

God the Creator shaped you into a family unlike any other that has ever been—or will be. *Be-good-to-your-family Therapy* shows you how to celebrate this precious gift.

1.

Remember the sacredness of your family relationship. God created you to be parent to these children, and God created them to be children to you. You bring to each other what no one else can.

2.

Your family is a wonder, the unique consequence of countless choices made over generations by all those who came before you—choices that resulted in each of you being here today. Celebrate the special, one-of-a-kind miracle of your family.

3.

Stories weave the fabric of family into a timeless tapestry. Turn off the TV, CD player, and video games—and tell your stories. You'll create your own spoken scriptures for future generations.

4.

Families gather to celebrate holidays, birthdays, anniversaries, special occasions. Use these milestones to create traditions, and use your traditions to build memories and connect hearts.

5.

Collect family memories in photos, videos, audiotapes, and scrapbooks, and then revisit the past together. Memories are links that join yesterday to today.

6.

Take time—at family meetings, at meals, in private chats—to talk, to listen, and to understand. Communication builds trust; trust binds.

7.

Play together as a family. Laughter and excitement release energy that enlivens and renews body and spirit. When the family plays together, everybody wins.

8.

Laughter is the heart's favorite exercise. Don't take yourselves—as individuals and as a family—too seriously. Act silly, tell jokes, and remember funny family stories.

9.

Welcome the unplanned moment into your family; leave room for spontaneity and serendipity. The unexpected is where we find some of life's sweetest gifts.

10.

Family means sharing responsibilities. Assign chores according to abilities, preferences, and time. Be flexible; rotate chores for variety. When the whole family chips in to do a big job, enjoy the team spirit and celebrate your accomplishment.

11.

Cultivate awe by noticing God's simple wonders—and point them out to each other: the delicate strands of a spiderweb, the tenacious grace of a dandelion, the squishiness of mud. The "wow" that comes from attending to life's fine details is truly a prayer of reverence.

12.

A healthy family strives for balance. When the demands of work, school, social activities, and church or civic responsibilities rob you of precious quality time your family needs, everyone suffers. Learn to say "no" so you can say "yes" to what matters most.

13.

Meals feed more than the body. Arrange your schedule to allow your family to come together regularly to share meals. Shared food and conversation is a blessing that nurtures both bodies and spirits.

14.

Build family faith by encouraging prayer: Sunday worship, mealtime prayer, informal moments in times of fear, sadness, or joy. Family prayer has the power to transform hearts, heal wounds, and restore peace.

15.

Loving touch goes deep—all the way to the soul. Use back pats, quick hugs, goodnight kisses, and delicate tickles to reassure, affirm, and comfort. Touch says "I love you" in countless ways.

16.

Develop simple family rituals to keep your hearts connected throughout the day. A goodbye kiss, a morning hug, a love note tucked in a lunch box can touch the spirit, generate smiles, warm the heart.

WEST HILL SCHOOL
Good luck with the play tryout! Love, mom
Good Luck with the play tryout. Love, mom

17.

Each family member is special in her or his own way. Appreciate the differences in ages, development levels, abilities, experiences, and limitations. They give your family variety, richness, substance, character, and strength.

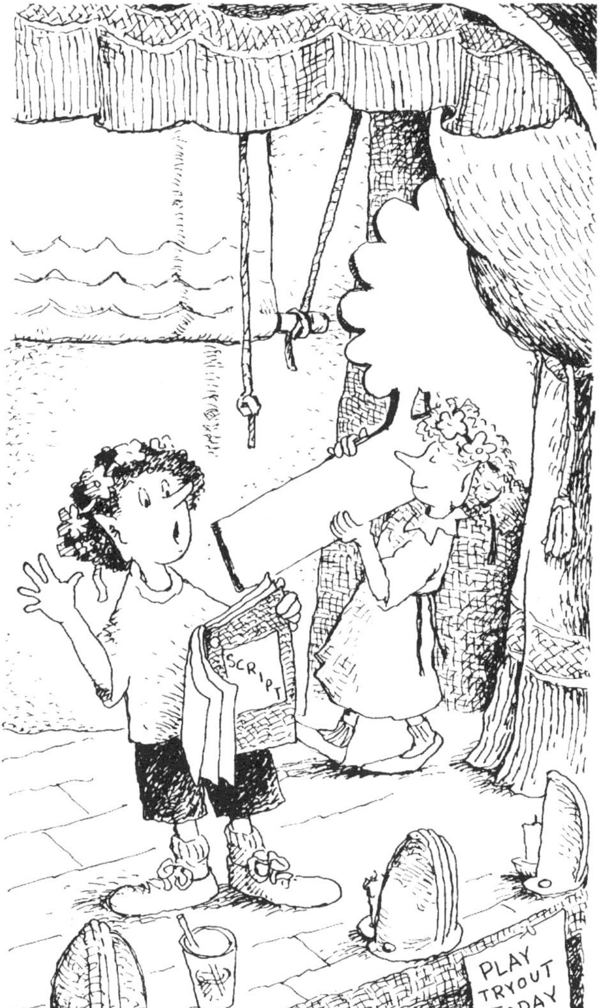
SCRIPT
PLAY
TRYOUT
TODAY

18.

The honors of one family member belong to all family members. Recognize strengths, affirm one another, be generous with praise, and share the spotlight.

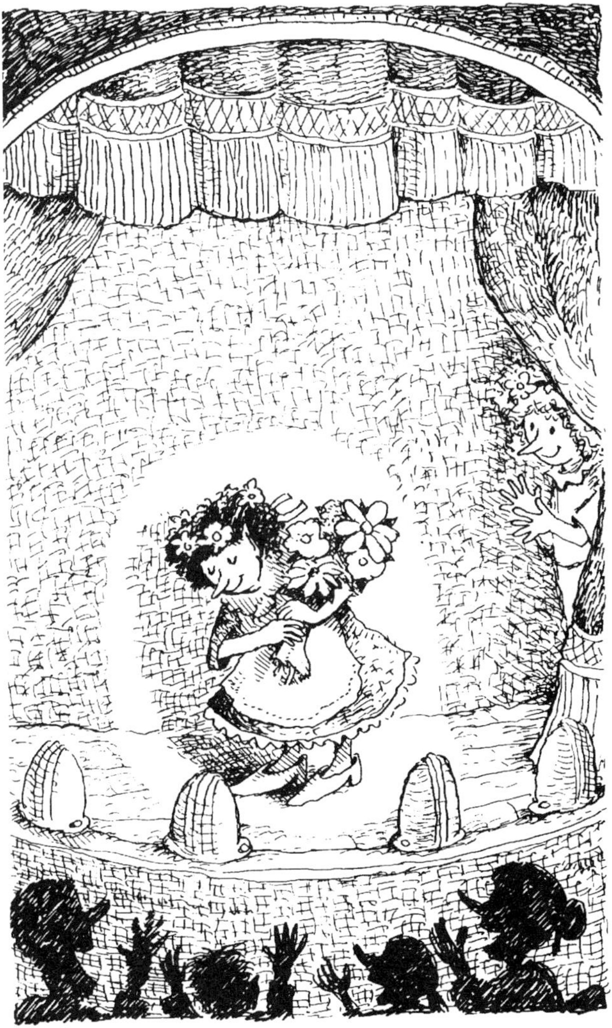

19.

Mistakes, misunderstandings, and disappointments are daily fare in family life. Examine expectations; don't demand perfection. Above all, be tolerant.

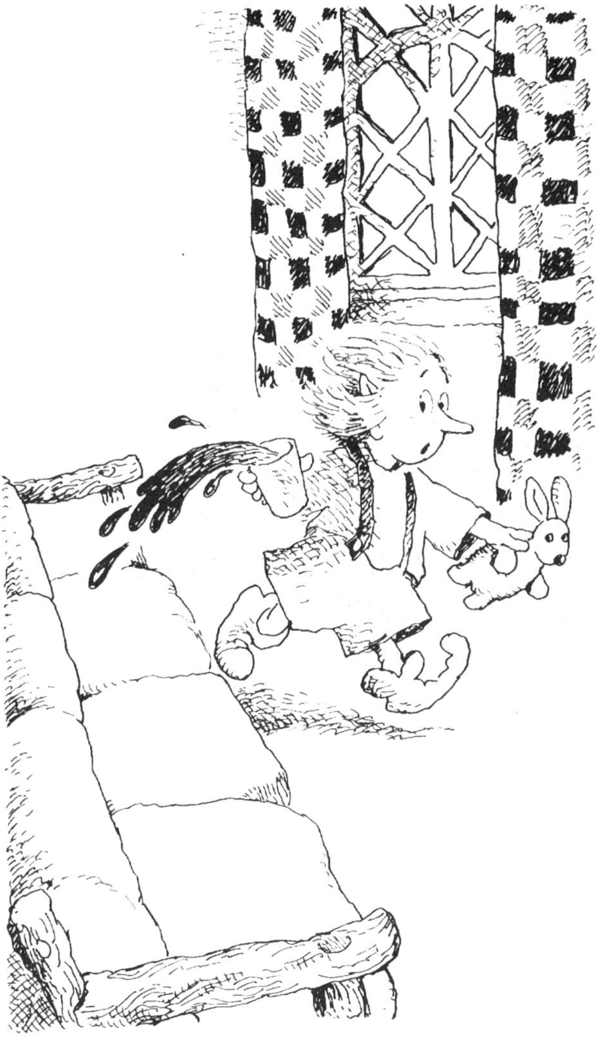

20.

You can still love family members even when you don't like what they've done. At those times, tell them you love them—and remind yourself as well.

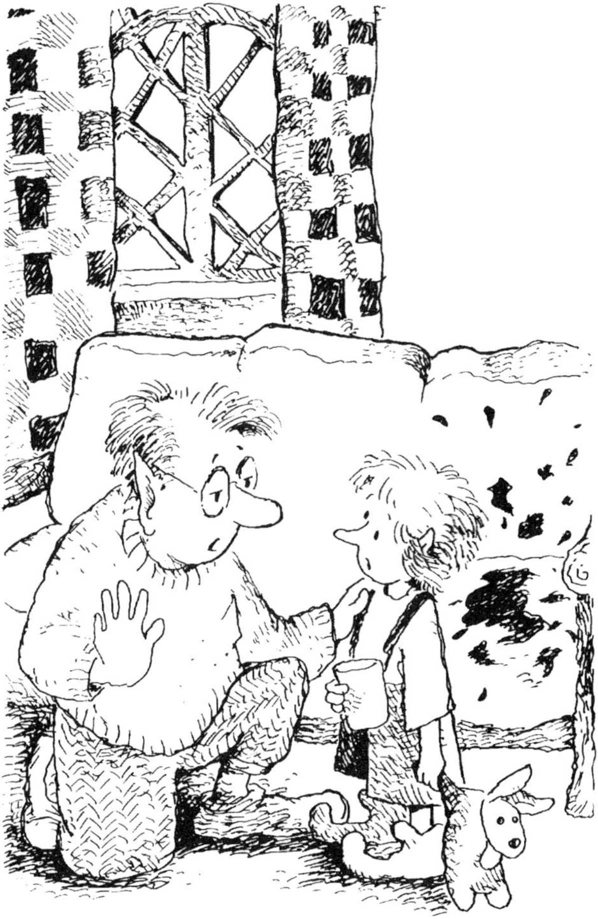

21.

Tears express who you are in your most intense moments. Let your family be a safe place for tears. Allow them to bring you the gifts of healing, peace, and closeness.

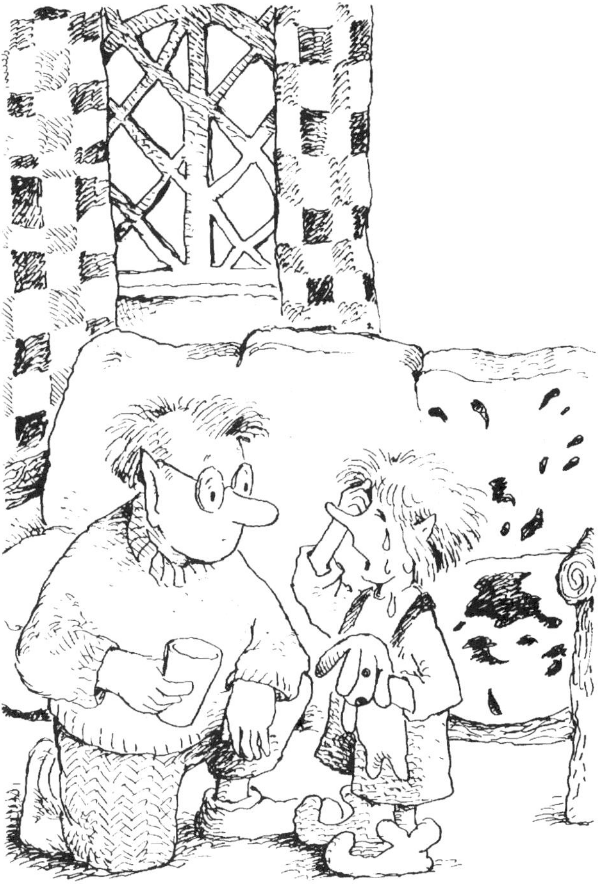

22.

Family life provides sacred opportunities to forgive and be forgiven. When tempers flare and feelings are hurt, say "I'm sorry" and "I forgive you," and you'll give love a fresh chance.

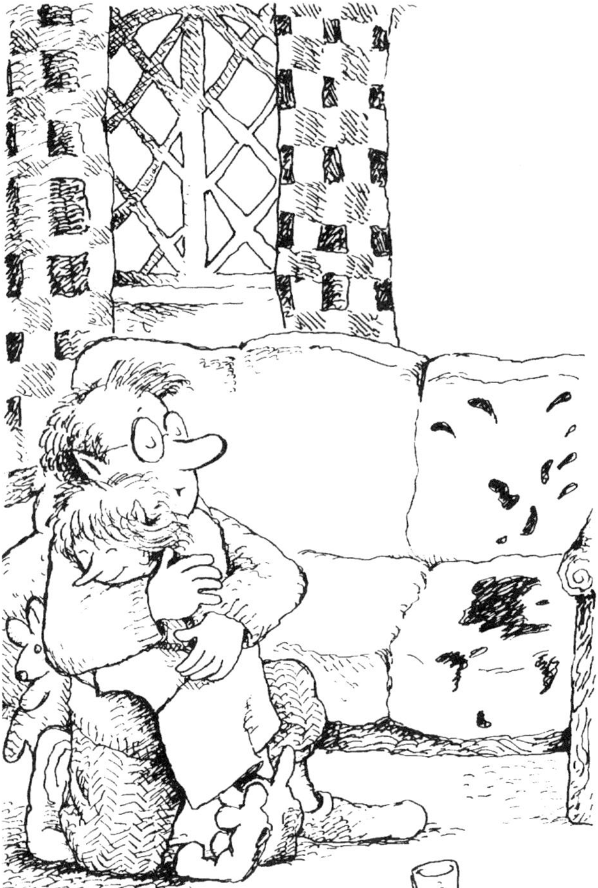

23.

Every member of the family has a different perspective. Relish the different feelings and views rather than trying to homogenize, stifle, or ignore them. You'll deepen your own experiences, intensify your awareness, and multiply your joy.

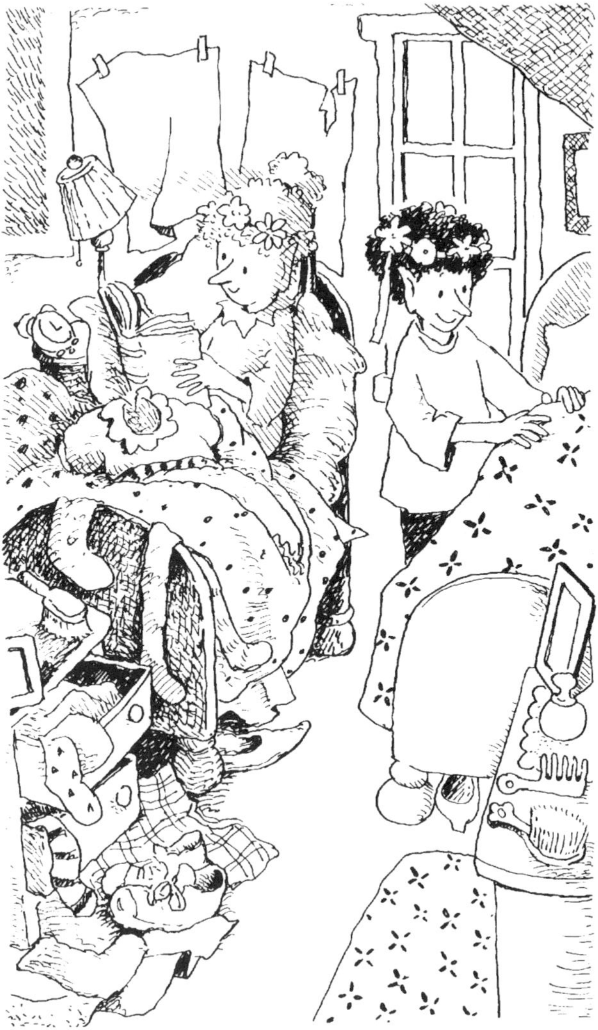

24.

Every family has conflict. But if you avoid blame, really listen, and try creative solutions, conflict can bring deeper understanding and appreciation for each member's distinctness.

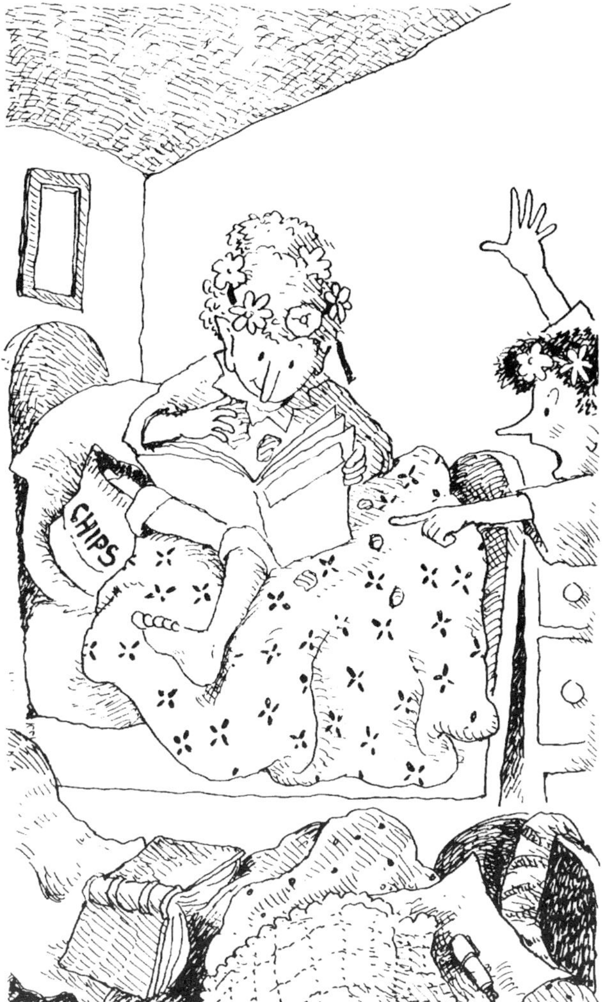
CHIPS

25.

Every family with more than one child experiences sibling rivalry. When a problem arises, let your fighting children sit across a table from each other (to eliminate physical contact) and work it out. When children see that a parent won't pick a side, they learn the value—and necessity—of compromise.

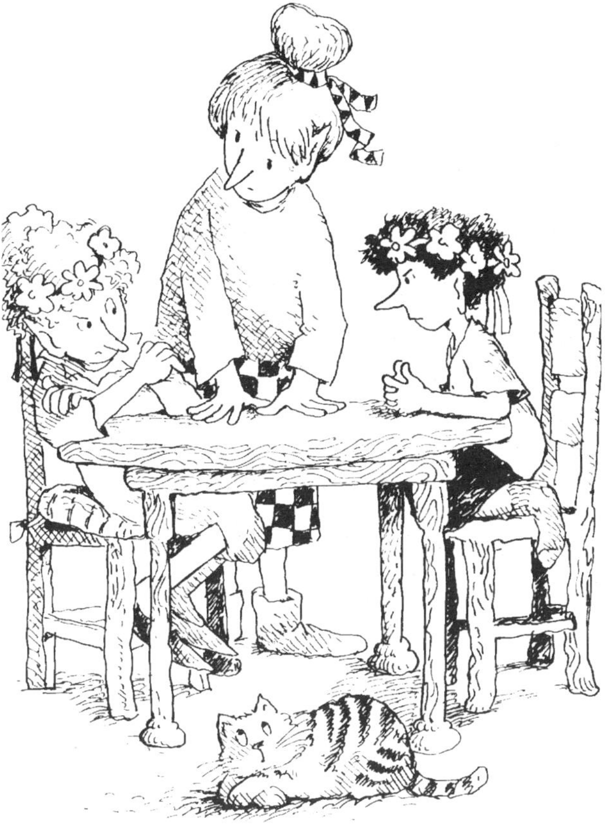

26.

Every family needs help from time to time. Be willing to tap into resources you can't provide for yourselves: read what wise people have written, join support groups, talk to a pastoral counselor, seek professional therapy.

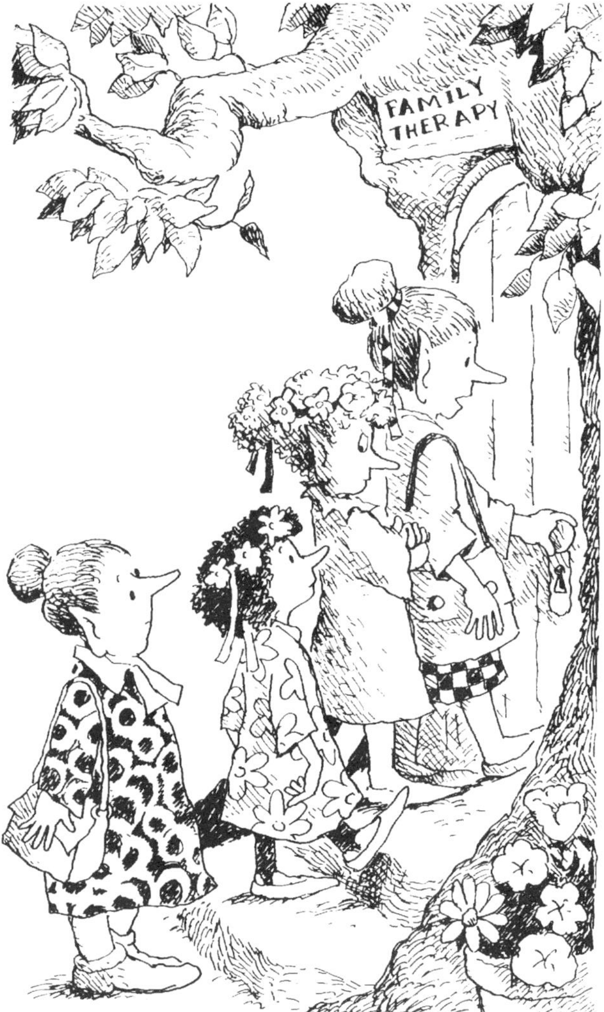
FAMILY
THERAPY

27.

Plan, set goals, and dream about the future together. Talking about what you'd like to do, where you'd like to go, what you'd like to be as a family deepens your sense of identity, solidarity, and purpose.

HOME WISH LIST
Bigger Kitchen
Bigger Yard
2 Bathrooms
MY own Room !
FOR SALE
SALE
HOMES F
HOMES FOR SALE
SALE

28.

No family can operate without a budget—whether tight or loosely defined. Let everyone know about the budget, to the degree he or she can understand. Sharing information about family finances helps everyone separate "needs" from "wants" when setting priorities.

HOME WISH
LIST

MY OWN ROOM
MY OWN CLOSET
MY OWN POOL
MY OWN HOUSE
MY OWN BARN
FOR MY OWN
HORSE

29.

Families become better, wiser, stronger by taking risks. Encourage risk and minimize fear by defining success as learning and growth and by assuring mutual support.

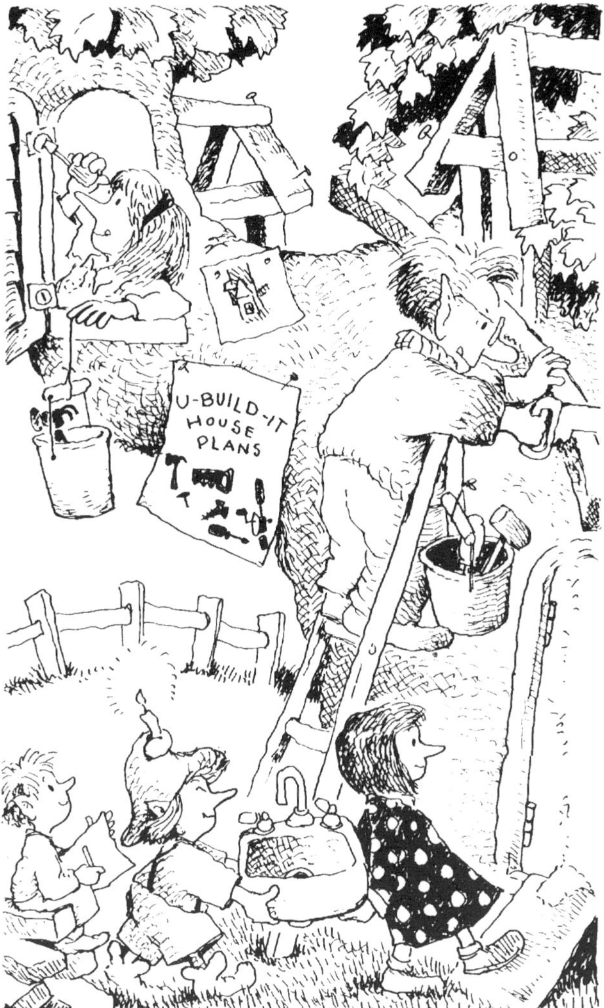
U-BUILD-IT
HOUSE
PLANS

30.

Families change: they relocate, welcome new members, and grieve the loss of those who die. Notice and respect change. Allow expressions of sadness, disappointment, anger—and talk about how to adjust. The family that changes together grows together.

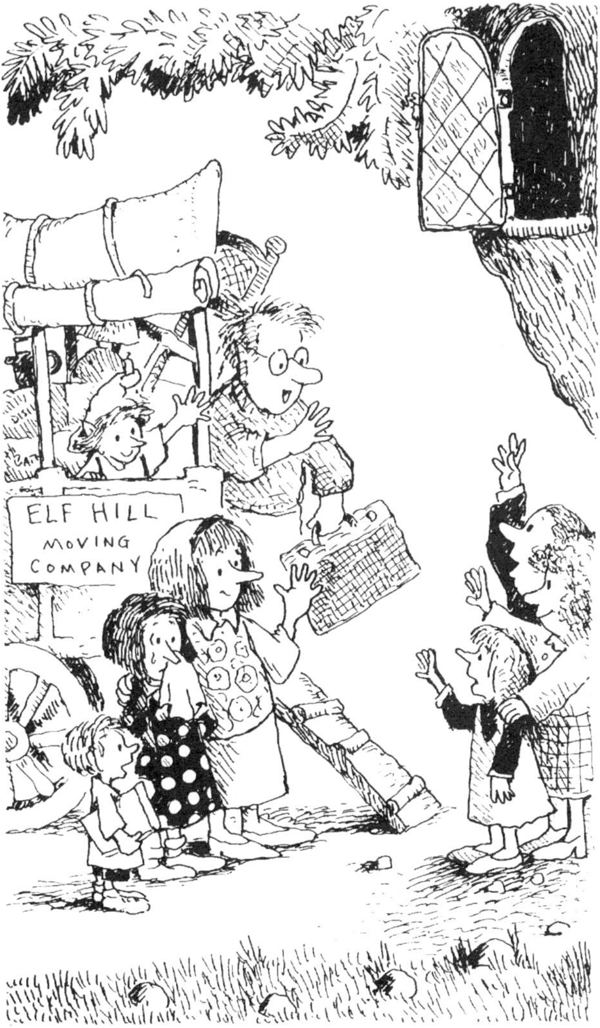
ELF HILL
MOVING
COMPANY

31.

Your time apart from one another is as important as your time together. Allow family members to take private personal time to be alone with themselves and God. Time alone quiets the mind and enriches the soul, making time together as a family more meaningful.

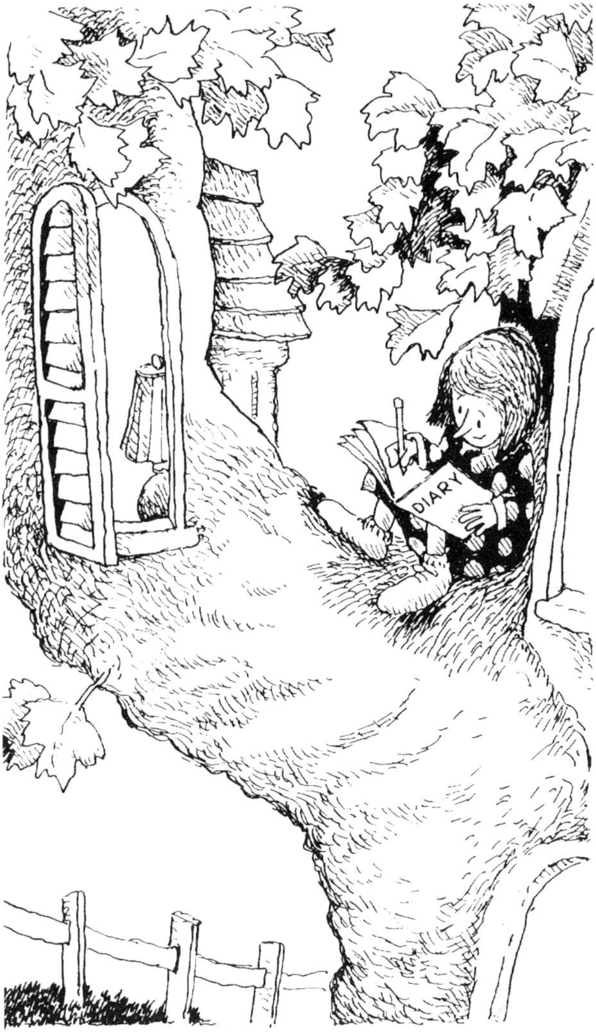
DIARY

32.

Personal things and space are sacred. Respect one another's need, right, and privilege to define personal territory. It's one important way individuality takes shape.

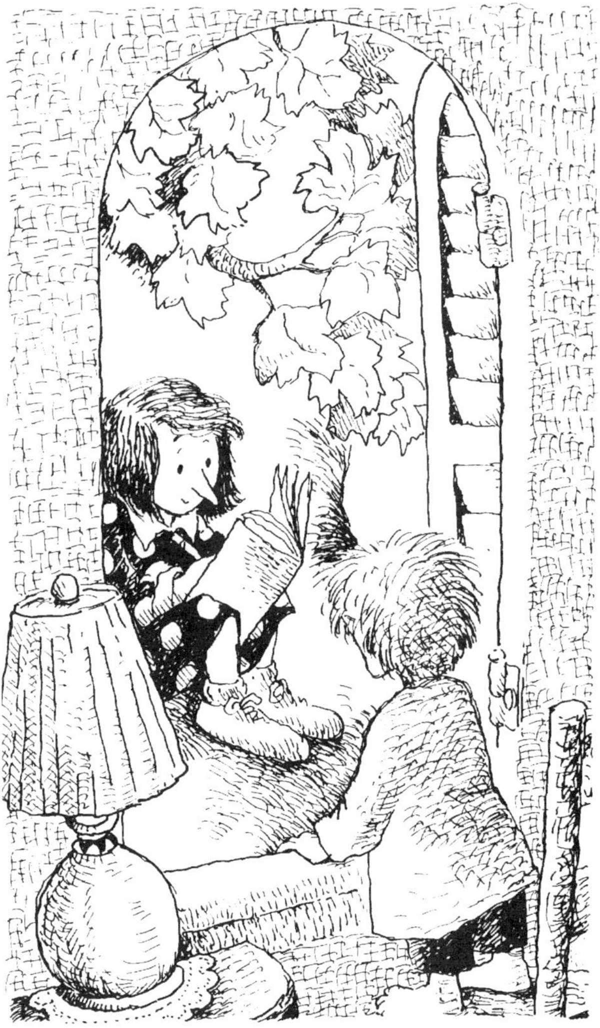

33.

Family is at its best in harmony with Mother Earth. Become earth-friendly by consuming less, recycling, planting a tree, using public transportation. Your family's care of the earth can enhance the future of generations to come.

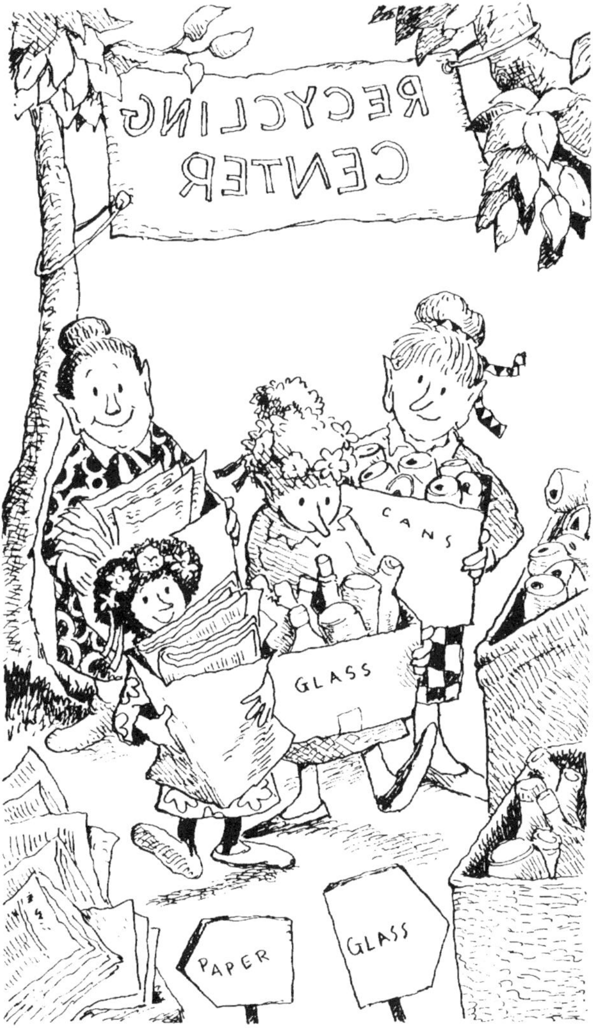
RECYCLING
CENTER
CANS
GLASS
PAPER
GLASS

34.

Open your home to friends, both old and new. They'll expand your awareness, challenge your preconceptions, bring you delight.

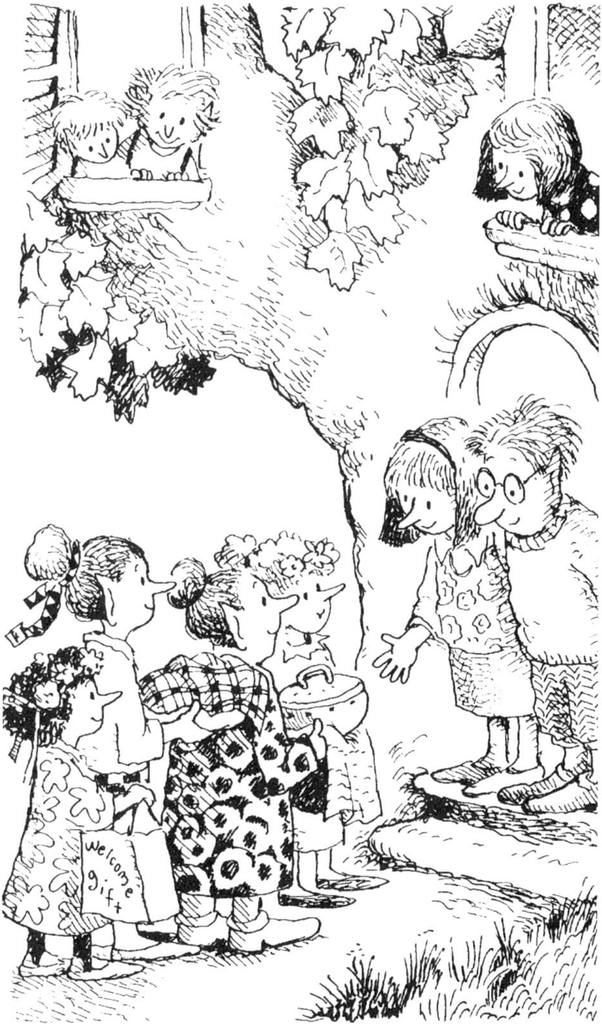
Welcome gift

35.

Help your family accept and celebrate the diversity of our "world family." Intolerance, bigotry, hostility, and fear of differences are learned or prevented within the family.

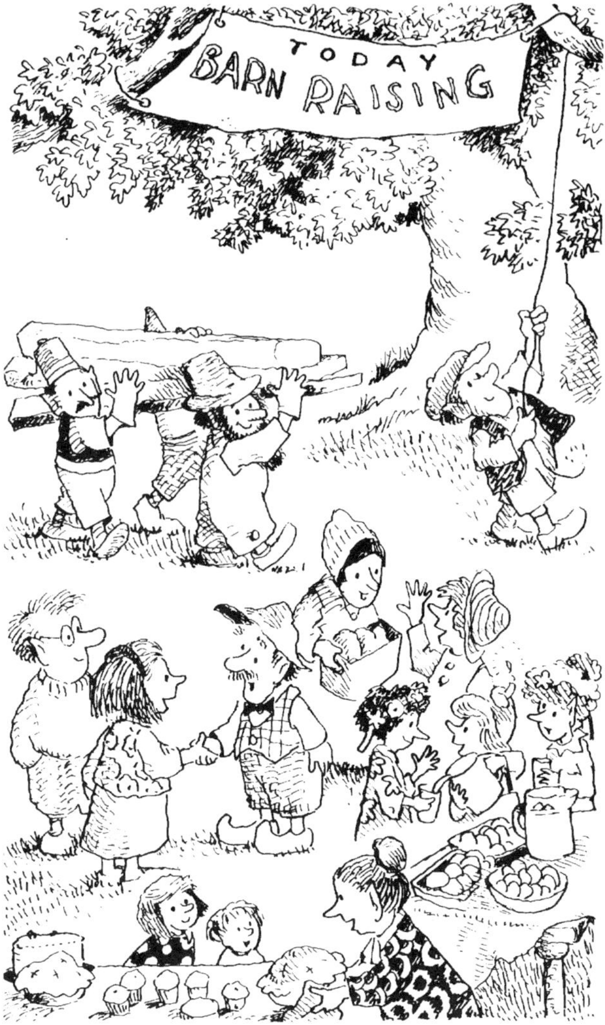
TODAY
BARN RAISING

36.

Use your power as a family to make a difference. Together you can respond to the needs of your neighbors, your community, your country, your world.

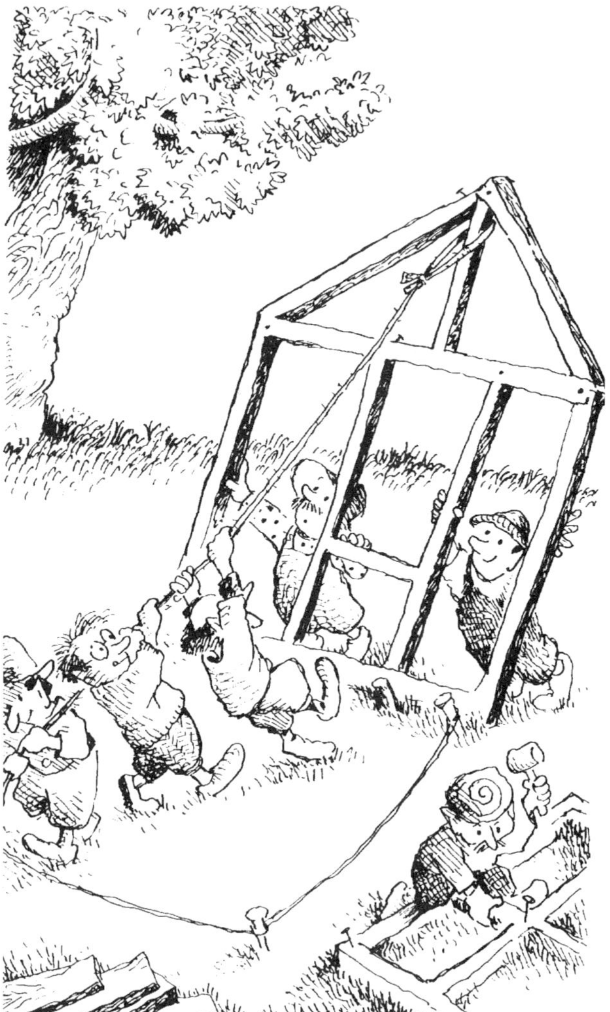

37.

This present, never-to-be-repeated moment with your family is the moment that matters. Don't miss it.

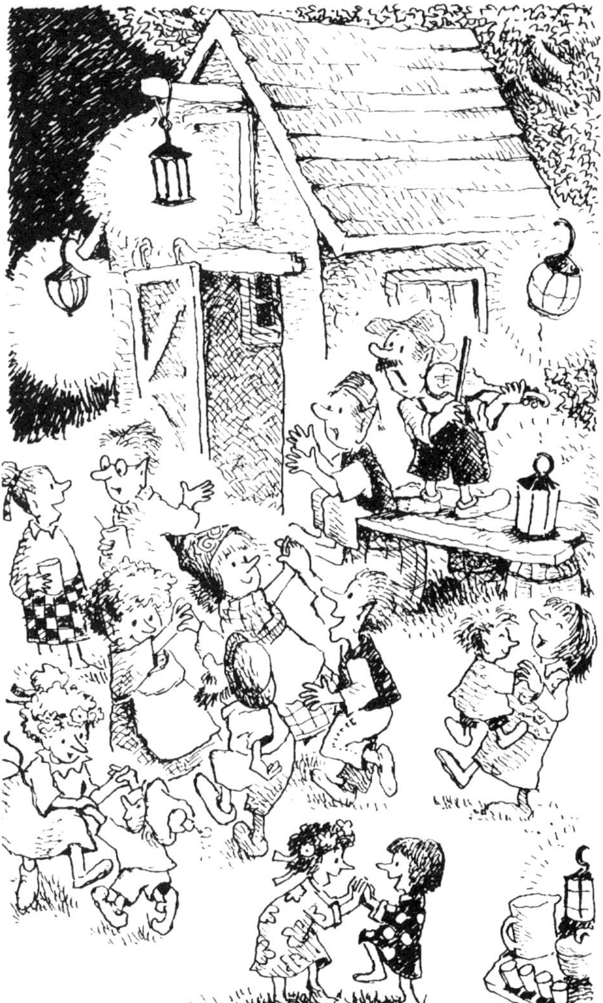

38.

God the Creator brought the gift of family into the world. Celebrate your Creator as the very Love that resides at the heart of your family.

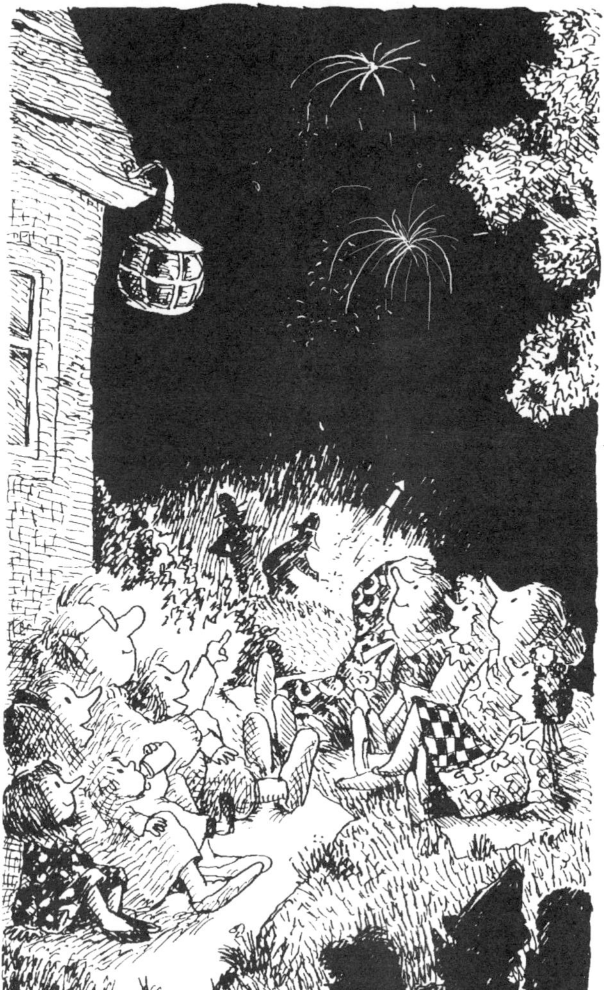

Kass Dotterweich, the mother of six children, lives with her family in St. Louis, Missouri. She is a managing editor for Liguori Publications and the author of *You Break It, You Buy It—and Three Dozen More Opportune Moments to Teach Family Values.*

Illustrator for the Abbey Press Elf-help Books, **R.W. Alley** also illustrates and writes children's books. He lives in Barrington, Rhode Island, with his wife, daughter, and son.

The Story of the Abbey Press Elves

The engaging figures that populate the Abbey Press "elf-help" line of publications and products first appeared in 1987 on the pages of a small self-help book called *Be-good-to-yourself Therapy*. Shaped by the publishing staff's vision and defined in R.W. Alley's inventive illustrations, they lived out author Cherry Hartman's gentle, self-nurturing advice with charm, poignancy, and humor.

Reader response was so enthusiastic that more Elf-help Books were soon under way, a still-growing series that has inspired a line of related gift products.

The especially endearing character featured in the early books—sporting a cap with a mood-changing candle in its peak—has since been joined by a spirited female elf with flowers in her hair.

These two exuberant, sensitive, resourceful, kindhearted, lovable sprites, along with their lively elfin community, reveal what's truly important as they offer messages of joy and wonder, playfulness and co-creation, wholeness and serenity, the miracle of life and the mystery of God's love.

With wisdom and whimsy, these little creatures with long noses demonstrate the elf-help way to a rich and fulfilling life.

Elf-help Books

...adding "a little character" and a lot of help to self-help reading!

Be-good-to-your-family Therapy
#20154 $4.95   ISBN 0-87029-300-1

Stress Therapy
#20153 $4.95   ISBN 0-87029-301-X

Making-sense-out-of-suffering Therapy
#20156 $4.95   ISBN 0-87029-296-X

Get Well Therapy
#20157 $4.95   ISBN 0-87029-297-8

Anger Therapy
#20127 $4.95   ISBN 0-87029-292-7

Caregiver Therapy
#20164 $4.95   ISBN 0-87029-285-4

Self-esteem Therapy
#20165 $4.95   ISBN 0-87029-280-3

Take-charge-of-your-life Therapy
#20168 $4.95   ISBN 0-87029-271-4

Work Therapy
#20166 $4.95   ISBN 0-87029-276-5

Everyday-courage Therapy
#20167 $4.95   ISBN 0-87029-274-9

Peace Therapy
#20176 $4.95   ISBN 0-87029-273-0

Friendship Therapy
#20174 $4.95   ISBN 0-87029-270-6

Christmas Therapy (color edition)
#20175 $5.95   ISBN 0-87029-268-4

Grief Therapy
#20178 $4.95   ISBN 0-87029-267-6

More Be-good-to-yourself Therapy
#20180 $3.95   ISBN 0-87029-262-5

Happy Birthday Therapy
#20181 $4.95   ISBN 0-87029-260-9

Forgiveness Therapy
#20184 $4.95   ISBN 0-87029-258-7

Keep-life-simple Therapy
#20185 $4.95   ISBN 0-87029-257-9

Be-good-to-your-body Therapy
#20188 $4.95   ISBN 0-87029-255-2

Celebrate-your-womanhood Therapy
#20189 $4.95   ISBN 0-87029-254-4

Acceptance Therapy (color edition)
#20182 $5.95   ISBN 0-87029-259-5

Acceptance Therapy
#20190 $4.95   ISBN 0-87029-245-5

Keeping-up-your-spirits Therapy
#20195 $4.95   ISBN 0-87029-242-0

Play Therapy
#20200 $4.95   ISBN 0-87029-233-1

Slow-down Therapy
#20203 $4.95   ISBN 0-87029-229-3

One-day-at-a-time Therapy
#20204 $4.95   ISBN 0-87029-228-5

Prayer Therapy
#20206 $4.95   ISBN 0-87029-225-0

Be-good-to-your-marriage Therapy
#20205 $4.95   ISBN 0-87029-224-2

Be-good-to-yourself Therapy (hardcover)
#20196 $10.95   ISBN 0-87029-243-9

Be-good-to-yourself Therapy
#20255 $4.95   ISBN 0-87029-209-9

Available at your favorite bookstore or directly from us at: One Caring Place, Abbey Press Publications, St. Meinrad, IN 47577. Or call 1-800-325-2511.